SPORTS HEROES AND LEGENDS

Mickey Mantle

D0729662

Read all of the books in this exciting,
action-packed biography series!

SPORTS HEROES AND LEGENDS

Mickey Mantle

by John Marlin

BARNES
& NOBLE
BOOKS

NEW YORK

For John and Joanne, who were with us
on August 26, 2002

Cover photograph:
© Bettmann/CORBIS

Copyright © 2004 by Lerner Publications Company

This first edition published by Barnes & Noble Publishing, Inc., by arrangement with Lerner Publications Company, a division of Lerner Publishing Group, Minneapolis, MN.

Barnes & Noble Publishing, Inc.
122 Fifth Avenue
New York, NY 10011

Written by Liesa Abrams

Sports Heroes and Legends™ is a trademark of Barnes & Noble Publishing, Inc.

ISBN 0-7607-5064-5

Printed and bound in the United States of America

04 05 06 07 08 BP 10 9 8 7 6 5 4 3 2 1

Contents

The Washington Wallop

April 17, 1953, was the two-year anniversary of Mickey Mantle's first major-league baseball game with the New York Yankees. Mickey had come a long way in those two years. The previous fall, he'd been the key player when the Yankees beat out their local rival, the Brooklyn Dodgers, for the 1952 World Series. Even the Dodgers' own star, Jackie Robinson, had told reporters, "He was the difference between the two clubs. . . . It was Mickey Mantle who killed us."

Mickey, just twenty-one years old, was proud of his accomplishments so far with the Yankees, but he always wanted more. He wanted to blast records, to be the standout player his father had always dreamed he would be.

On that April day, Mickey and his team were in Washington, D.C., playing against the Washington Senators at Griffith Stadium. Mickey came to bat, facing Washington's pitcher Chuck Stobbs. *I can do this*, he told himself as he waited for the pitch to come his way. *I can send this ball to the sky*.

Mickey was already known for power hitting and for racking up homers. But when Mickey's bat connected with Stobbs's pitch that day with a satisfying crack, it was like nothing Mickey or any baseball player or fan had ever seen before.

The entire stadium watched in amazement as the ball soared through the air across left field, traveling so fast and so high that the Senators' left fielder didn't even budge. He stood rooted to the spot, frozen in awe like everyone else.

While Mickey ran the bases, his ball kept going, sailing right over the fifty-five-foot-high wall behind the left-field bleachers—something that had never been done before. The ball ricocheted off a sign on the stadium's scoreboard that was sixty feet high and about 460 feet from home plate. It finally landed in the yard of a nearby home.

Fans murmured, "Wow—not possible." This kid had unbelievable power! By the time the ball had reached its final destination, it was measured as having flown a mind-blowing 565 feet.

Mickey was swept up in a wave of excitement as everyone around him went crazy. They were sure they'd just witnessed the longest home run ever hit in major-league baseball. The hit was soon nicknamed the "Washington Wallop," and it started a new phenomenon known as the "tape-measure home run."

These homers traveled such incredible distances that they needed to be measured for the record books.

The Washington Wallop was a first for Mickey and the world of baseball. Mickey made himself an important promise that day—it wouldn't be the last time he wowed the world!

Chapter One

Born for Baseball

In 1931 catcher Gordon "Mickey" Cochrane of the Philadelphia Athletics finished the season with an impressive .349 batting average, making his number one fan, Elvin "Mutt" Mantle, proud. That same year, when Mutt found out that his wife, Lovell, was expecting their first baby, he made up his mind. "If my child is a boy," he told friends, "he's going to be a baseball player." Mutt was ready and willing to help destiny along, starting with giving his son the right name: Mickey!

Mickey Charles Mantle was born on October 20, 1931, in Spavinaw, Oklahoma. Mutt put his plan into action before Mickey's very first day in the world was over. "Mama says Dad showed me a baseball before I was twelve hours old and it almost broke his heart when I paid more attention to the bottle," Mickey recalled.

Mutt Mantle was more than just a passionate fan of baseball. He played the game he loved whenever he could, including spending some time on a semiprofessional baseball squad. As a young man, he had dreamed of playing professionally but was never given the chance. Mutt—like his father, his brothers, and other relatives—worked in the mines, which was the only employment choice for many people living in that area during the hard economic times of the Great Depression. When Mutt wasn't working, though, his focus was on making sure his son could live out the baseball dreams he himself hadn't been able to pursue.

❝ *I was probably the only baby in history whose first lullaby was the radio broadcast of a ball game.* ❞

—MICKEY MANTLE

The Mantle family grew when twins Roy and Ray were born, and Mutt was pleased to find a better-paying mining job in Commerce, Oklahoma, about fifty miles from Spavinaw. Mickey was four when his dad brought the family to Commerce, where they were living when Mickey's sister, Barbara, and youngest brother, Larry "Butch" Mantle, were born.

Mickey and Mutt weren't the only ones who loved baseball. The Mantles were definitely a baseball family. Their favorite team was the St. Louis Cardinals, who played about 300 miles away in Missouri. Every day Lovell would listen to the radio broadcasts of the Cardinals' games, taking notes on the plays. That night over dinner with her husband and children, she would recount the action of the game as if they were all there together, watching it happen right in front of them! Still, even if Mickey wasn't the only fan, it was always Mickey whom Mutt believed would be the baseball star and Mickey who was being carefully groomed.

Every afternoon when Mickey finished school, he would come straight home to meet his father and grandfather, Charlie Mantle, for batting practice. Mutt and Charlie hurried home from the mines to be ready for Mickey, making his baseball lessons their top priority. Mickey didn't mind one bit—he loved baseball as much as his father did and looked forward to their practice sessions. "Once I learned to hit a ball with a bat," Mickey said, "I needed none of my father's urging to play the game."

❝ *What [kept] me driving hard, from the time that I was ten, to hit the ball better and farther was first of all my own love for the game and then my love for my father. I knew from the time I was small that every small victory I won, and every solid hit I made or prize I was awarded, brought real joy to my father's heart.*❞
—MICKEY MANTLE

Mickey did dread one part of these lessons. He was a naturally strong right-handed hitter, which meant he could hit best from a left-handed pitcher like his grandfather. But Mutt believed if he could give his son enough early experience also hitting left-handed, then Mickey would grow up able to hit well from either side of home plate. That way he'd be what's called a switch-hitter, a double threat against any opponent. Mutt was convinced that switch-hitting was possible for any good player to learn with practice and that it would prove to be a key talent for Mickey. Luckily, Mutt Mantle happened to pitch right-handed, so Mutt and Charlie would take turns pitching to little Mickey. At first Mickey was frustrated. Hitting left-handed was so hard!

Mickey wasn't so off base when he called his father a "prophet" for teaching him how to switch-hit. In 1951, Mickey's first year with the Yankees, ten major-league switch-hitters were playing. By 1971, thanks to Mickey's successful example, there were forty-one!

But his dad wouldn't take no for an answer, and eventually Mickey learned to hit from the left side nearly as well as he could from the right.

The hard work started to pay off when ten-year-old Mickey

joined what was then called a Pee Wee League team in the nearby mining town of Douthat. Mickey played catcher, like his namesake, but he was very small for the position. "When he squatted down behind the batter wearing that [chest] protector that was too big for him, you couldn't see his feet," recalled Lovell Mantle. "About all you could see of him—except for his arms—were those two little eyes sticking out of the protector like a scared turtle looking out of its shell." But Mickey's size didn't stop him from showing what he could do at bat. With Mickey leading the charge, the Douthat team made it all the way to the Pee Wee Division Championship and won the title!

Mickey knew this was just the beginning. If he wanted to see his father's dream for him come true, he had to keep playing his hardest. He had to stay hungry for the next win.

Mickey's focus never left that goal, and the following year he went out for the Junior Cardinal League, even though the minimum age for the league was twelve and Mickey was still only eleven. The team from the neighboring town of Picher was so eager to have Mickey that they convinced the league to waive the age rule, and Mickey picked up where he'd left off on the Douthat team, impressing local fans with his strong hits.

Where Mickey *didn't* impress was in his role as catcher. He played the position decently, but the coach felt his amazing leg speed was being wasted. So in Mickey's second season with the

Picher team, he was switched to second base. Mutt couldn't help feeling disappointed since he'd always imagined his son as a catcher, like his namesake. But he realized the coach was right. Playing second base would allow Mickey to really showcase more of his talents.

Mickey couldn't get enough of baseball, and he joined every team he could. The local Gabby Street League (named after major-league player Gabby Street) gave Mickey a chance to play again for Douthat. Mickey played alongside LeRoy Bennett and Nick Ferguson, friends from his neighborhood who loved baseball—almost!—as much as he did. Ferguson still remembers how impressed he was at everything Mickey could do back then. He says the three of them used to watch newsreels showing the St. Louis Browns' one-armed outfielder, Pete Gray, who could catch and throw the ball with the same arm. The boys would then try to imitate the ability themselves. "Mickey could actually do it, just like he had one arm," Ferguson marvels. "He coulda thrown left-handed for real if he ever had to."

Mickey was once again the star of the team, not only for his ace hitting but also for these other skills he seemed to develop so easily. Mickey even pitched for the Gabby Street team occasionally, and Ferguson remembers the squad winning some big games that Mickey pitched. The biggest win at stake for the team, of course, was the league championship. Soon enough, Mickey's Douthat team had come out on top!

---

66 *The difference between me and many other boys who played ball with just as much skill [was] that I had a father to encourage and push me.* 99

—MICKEY MANTLE

This championship was even more exciting for Mickey than his earlier one, especially because Gabby Street himself attended the banquet dinner held to celebrate the victory. It was clear that all the hard work Mickey, his dad, and his grandfather had put in was paying off, and Mickey relaxed and enjoyed one of the happiest periods of his life. Every day was filled with baseball, baseball, and more baseball, and he was surrounded by the family he loved more than anything. But just around the corner, the first tragedy of Mickey's young life was waiting.

Chapter Two

Close Call

Mickey's childhood wasn't always easy. His family never had much money, and Mickey spent countless hours and days forced to practice and sharpen his baseball skills. But to Mickey, free time and luxuries weren't important. Only baseball and his family were.

> Mickey first learned to count, at age three, by listening to Mutt count off the number of bases on a baseball diamond!

That's why it was especially hard on thirteen-year-old Mickey when he learned that his grandfather, Charlie, was very ill with Hodgkin's disease, a type of cancer. "Grandpa suddenly became old and feeble, almost overnight," Mickey remembered. It was scary for him to see the transformation in someone who had so recently appeared strong and healthy. The whole family watched as Charlie grew sicker and sicker.

Mutt Mantle was convinced that if his father could live somewhere with fresh air, away from the mines, Charlie would have a better chance of fighting the disease. So Mutt moved his family to a farm not too far from Commerce, where they could live on and farm 160 acres of land in exchange for sharing the crops with the landowner.

Farm life was new to Mickey and his siblings, but they pitched in and helped their parents with chores, enjoying much of the work. "We milked cows, we had pigs, we had chickens, we did it all," Mickey's brother Ray said. Mickey also remembered playing baseball out in the farm's huge pasture with his brothers and sister, who were finally old enough to join him in some pick-up games. And he even had a horse! Mickey's horse was named Tony, and he rode Tony to school every day. "He sure was an understanding horse," Mickey said. "He didn't like school either!"

Unfortunately, as happy as Mickey and the rest of his family were with farm life, Charlie was just too sick to recover. Mickey's beloved grandfather died not long after the family moved to the farm, and Mickey was devastated. "I never forgot that moment," Mickey said, "standing beside the casket with my little twin brothers, Ray and Roy, the three of us looking down on him, and my father whispering, 'Say good-bye to Grandpa.'"

It was Mickey's first brush with tragic loss but far from his last. In fact, Mickey lost two uncles to the same disease within years of Charlie Mantle's death, casting shadows over the lives of Mickey's father, Mickey, and his brothers as they wondered if more members of the family would later face the same illness.

Meanwhile Mutt Mantle had other, more pressing worries. He was learning that life on a farm meant being subject to the uncertainty of weather. One extremely wet summer caused him to lose all of his crops. He was forced to return to his job at the mines and move his family to a tiny, less expensive home in the town of Whitebird, on the fringes of Commerce. The Mantles were so poor that their new home initially didn't even have a kitchen or indoor plumbing. Mickey slept in a room with his parents and sister, while his three brothers squeezed into an adjoining bedroom.

❝ *The only thing I can do is play baseball. . . . It's the only thing I know.* ❞

—MICKEY MANTLE

How did Mickey deal with his harsh living conditions? By focusing on baseball, the one part of his life that had never let him down. Mickey continued to play with neighborhood friends. Every once in a while, when Mutt could scrape the money together, he'd bring Mickey along to a minor-league game in Kansas or Missouri. Mickey would watch the players in awe, dreaming of becoming one of them someday soon.

Mickey still had to get through high school, where he filled as much of his time as he could with sports since the academic side of school didn't interest him very much.

Mickey had started playing basketball in junior high, and he had gotten pretty good. At his basketball games, it was actually Lovell who would cheer the loudest from the sidelines—and who would lose her cool if she didn't like something that happened on the court. "If she objected to a referee's decision," Mickey said, "you could hear her voice travel across the gym: 'Where are your glasses, you bum!'"

Mutt supported his son at the games as well, but he couldn't help worrying about the dangers of playing other sports outside of baseball, especially the sport that he believed carried the most risk to Mickey's body—football. Mickey had his work cut out for him to convince his dad to let him join the Commerce High Tigers football squad. Eventually his pleas won, and Mickey became one of the rare players to stand out on all three high school teams—baseball, basketball, and football.

❝In my opinion, baseball was Mickey's second-best sport. He was the best high school football player I ever saw.❞

—MICKEY'S HIGH SCHOOL
FOOTBALL COACH, JOHN LINGO

Mickey's speed and strength helped him succeed in the three very different sports, and Mickey was thrilled to earn a starting position as a halfback for the football team his sophomore year. He knew that football was a rough game and that injuries came with the territory. When a teammate accidentally kicked him in the shin during an early season practice, Mickey barely noticed.

Until that night.

Mickey could barely sleep as the pain in his leg got worse and worse. The next morning, Mickey was horrified to look down and see that his deep blue ankle had swollen to twice its size! When Mickey showed his father, Mutt panicked and immediately brought his son to the closest hospital. The doctor believed it was some kind of infection but advised Mutt to take Mickey to the bigger hospital in Picher, where they had more advanced diagnostic equipment.

Doctors at the Picher hospital were able to identify more precisely what was wrong with Mickey, but the news wasn't good. Mickey had osteomyelitis, a bacterial infection of the bone that causes chronic inflammation. Apparently the blow to Mickey's shin had been so hard that it had exposed his bone to bacteria, which had led to the infection. To Mickey and Mutt, it didn't matter what had caused the problem. All they knew was that Mickey had an illness that could possibly keep him from ever stepping up to home plate again.

Mickey was crushed. "When it finally dawned on me that possibly I would be forced to forget about baseball, football, and any other sports," he said, "I thought I'd go crazy." Mutt and Lovell were just as concerned but determined to find an answer. Mutt drove Mickey to the Crippled Children's Hospital in Oklahoma City when it became clear that the doctors in Picher weren't able to help.

Mickey's weight had dropped from around 130 down to 110 pounds, and he spent his nights alone in the hospital, terrified and suffering from a high fever. At one point, the doctors warned they might have to amputate the leg to save Mickey's life. Mickey was desperate, but Lovell stood firm, telling the doctors there was no way they were taking her son's leg.

Then, amazingly, Mickey began to recover. Luckily for Mickey, a new drug called penicillin was beginning to be used to treat bacterial infections. Mickey had been receiving injections of penicillin since his stay at the hospital in Picher, but it wasn't until his stay at the Oklahoma City hospital that the shots finally began to work. Coincidentally Mickey's recovery seemed to begin right after Lovell declared that no one was operating on her son's leg. Mickey continued to improve and was released from the hospital on crutches just in time for the 1946 World Series.

Mutt knew that spending so much time lying helpless in a hospital bed had hurt his son not only physically but mentally, too. If there was one way to inspire Mickey to toss out the crutches, it was to remind him of his dreams—*their* dreams. So Mutt saved up his money and presented Mickey with a surprise road trip to St. Louis to watch the Cardinals face the Boston Red Sox in the World Series.

Mickey lit up, ecstatic at the opportunity. He and Mutt attended two games—the opener, which their team lost, and the next game, in which the Cardinals handed them a 3–0 victory to celebrate. Back in Commerce, Mickey was glued to the radio for the next five games as the series stretched to the last moment. It was game seven, and the series was on the line with Cardinals player Enos Slaughter on first base. As Mickey listened, breathless, Slaughter scored the winning run all the way from first base on a single, clinching the game and the series for the Cardinals.

Mickey began cheering like crazy, then realized he could

learn something from Slaughter's awesome play, from the way he had gone up against tough odds and come out a winner.

"Burn the crutches," Mickey told his parents. "I'm going to play ball."

Chapter Three

The Windup

By the spring of 1947, Mickey had come a long way. He had mostly recovered from his illness, but he was still working hard to regain his strength. He joined a youth team from Miami, Oklahoma, and started getting back into shape the only way he knew how—on the baseball field.

In his junior year of high school, Mickey was so fired up to return to the world of sports that he even resumed playing football. This time he made it through the season without any

Mickey switched off between playing shortstop and pitcher for his high school baseball team during his junior year. In one game as pitcher, he struck out fourteen batters!

serious injuries and played so well, he was named to the all-district team. Next came a winter on the varsity basketball team. And spring meant Mickey could get back into the swing of things in his very favorite sport—baseball.

Along with playing for the Commerce High squad, Mickey was also recruited to play for the Whiz Kids, a team with a home base in Baxter Springs, Kansas. On the Whiz Kids, Mickey's position was once again switched, this time from second base to shortstop. The Whiz Kids were part of the same Ban Johnson League as the Miami team Mickey had played on in 1947, but the Whiz Kids were a much more competitive semiprofessional team, made up mostly of players at least eighteen years old. Whiz Kids coach Barney Barnett had noticed Mickey's strong playing in a game against Miami the previous spring, and he had a feeling about that Mantle kid. "Mickey," he told him, "the big leagues seem like a million miles from here and out of reach. But if you work real hard, they're not out of reach for you."

Mickey, at sixteen, was the youngest guy on the Whiz Kids squad. But he was also clearly the best. "He was a boy playing with men," recalled one childhood friend of Mickey's, "and he was better than all of them."

Word of Mickey's power and speed started to spread, and fans swarmed to Baxter Springs to watch this true Whiz Kid at bat. One summer night, Mickey's playing impressed the crowd of several hundred fans so much that it actually got him into trouble! He was on a roll that night and hit three home runs—one of them left-handed. All three sailed into the river that bordered right and center field. After the third and most powerful homer, one fan started to pass around a hat to collect donations for Mickey. Eager to show the young star how much they appreciated him, fans tossed in their change. In the end, Mickey was awarded with the total—fifty-three dollars, a pretty hefty sum for a teenager in the late 1940s. "More money than I had ever seen in one pile in my whole life," Mickey said.

> 66 *The most proud I ever was [was] when I . . . played on the Baxter Springs Whiz Kids. [They] gave me a uniform and . . . it was the first one my mom hadn't made for me. It was really something.* 99
>
> —MICKEY MANTLE, IN HIS 1974
> HALL OF FAME INDUCTION SPEECH

Sounds like a good thing, right? Well, unfortunately, it wasn't. At least, not after the Oklahoma State Athletic Commission, which regulated high school sports, heard about the incident. They ruled that since Mickey had accepted money, he was no longer an amateur player. That meant high school sports were off-limits for good!

Mickey was frantic, unable to think about giving up sports for his entire senior year of high school. But Mutt took care of the problem, working out a deal that allowed the ruling to be overturned as long as Mickey repaid the money. Whew!

The fall of his senior year, Mickey was back on the Commerce High football team and again played well enough to stand out on the squad. In fact, Mickey was even recruited to play college football. Mickey was flattered and excited at the attention, but there was never a question in his mind about the path he had ahead. He had never liked school very much, and he wasn't interested in college. His sights were set on just one thing: making it to the major leagues. It was all about baseball for Mickey Mantle.

As graduation approached, that goal seemed closer all the time. Mickey continued to improve with the Whiz Kids, and his body was finally filling out after all the weight he'd lost during his bout with osteomyelitis. What he didn't realize was that his excellent playing in Baxter Springs was being noticed by more than just the local fans. It had also caught the attention of major-league scouts and was already sealing the fate of his professional career.

It's a bit uncertain exactly when New York Yankees scout Tom Greenwade first made contact with Mickey and Mutt Mantle and raised the possibility of Mickey becoming a Yankee. It is certain, however, that Greenwade first saw Mickey play with the Whiz Kids, and he sure liked what he saw! According to some versions of the story, Greenwade spoke to Mickey after seeing him hit one of his classic homers at the first Whiz Kids game he attended. Some say Greenwade was so intent on snagging Mickey for the Yankees that he encouraged Mickey's high school principal to leak a false rumor that Mickey's injury had left him with bad legs, limiting his baseball future. Hugh Alexander, who was then the scout for the Cleveland Indians, claims he was given this information and it's why he didn't pursue the Mickey Mantle prospect any further. It could also explain why the St. Louis Cardinals' scout, who initially seemed interested in Mickey, eventually dropped out of sight and never approached Mickey or Mutt again after their first contact. While the Cardinals were Mickey and Mutt's favorite team, they hadn't offered a guarantee, as Mickey says Tom Greenwade had. And Mutt wanted to be certain that his son was heading to the major leagues.

Did Tom Greenwade assure Mickey and Mutt, as Mickey remembers, that if they waited for it, a contract with the Yankees was a sure bet the second Mickey had his diploma in hand? Or did Greenwade wait until Mickey's graduation to make the offer, following the rules of the scouting world that prohibit any contact between scouts and players until graduation, as Greenwade says he did? No one will ever know the truth. One thing is certain—the words *New York Yankees* were a beautiful sound to Mutt Mantle's ears. The Yankees had been brought to stardom by players of the past like Babe Ruth and Lou Gehrig, and at the time Greenwade came to Mickey, Yankee dynamo Joe DiMaggio was busy making headlines. The Yankees *were* baseball in America, and Mutt was so enchanted at the idea of his son wearing their uniform that he didn't question the small sum Greenwade proposed for Mickey's first season. Mickey would begin with one of the Yankees' Class D minor-league teams—the lowest-ranked team of the minor leagues, which start at D and go up to AAA.

Mickey would receive only a $400 salary, along with a $1,100 signing bonus, to sign up with the Yankees franchise. As Greenwade recalls, Mutt seemed more concerned with where Mickey would spend the summer than how much he would be paid. "We had two Class D teams, one in McAlester, Oklahoma, and one in Independence, Kansas. His father wanted him to go to Independence because it was closer to Commerce." The deal was done, and soon it was official. Mickey had a contract with the Yankees, and he was off to Independence, Kansas, to start playing minor-league ball.

Mickey was bursting with excitement, but the transition wasn't easy and neither was the first significant separation he'd ever had from his father. While Independence was the closest location to Commerce, it was still seventy miles away. "I have never met anyone who was any homesicker than I was my first days in Independence," Mickey said. "For a time I seriously thought I would give up the whole deal and go back to playing ball around Commerce."

But as much as Mickey missed his father, he knew just how disappointed Mutt would be if his son turned up on his doorstep, and he was determined to make things work in Independence. Things didn't get off to a great start, however. After about a month with the team, Mickey was hitting in the low .200s. He was also having trouble throwing the ball from his position as shortstop and catching fly balls. Could Mickey make it as a pro ballplayer?

MISSED TRYOUT

Mickey might not have ended up a Yankee if it hadn't rained so hard during a special tryout camp held by the St. Louis Browns—the less successful of the two St. Louis major-league teams—during Mickey's senior year. Mutt drove to St. Louis with Mickey, but the tryout was canceled because of the downpour, so the Browns never saw what Mickey had to offer.

After the uncertain start, Mickey improved, becoming more comfortable with his teammates and new life. By the end of the season, his average was up to .313—enough to show he had promise but not enough to send him up to the majors just yet.

MUSCLE MAN

Mickey was always known for his incredibly muscular arms, which helped him hit the ball with such force. He actually developed those huge muscles working in the mines with his father, where among other tasks he had to smash large rocks into small stones with a sledgehammer, called being a "screen ape."

In the fall of 1949, an unexpected threat appeared to Mickey's baseball career. Like lots of young American men, he received a notice in the mail instructing him to report for a physical examination with his local draft board. Trouble was brewing in Korea, and the U.S. Army needed to fill out its ranks. The physical was one test he was afraid to pass because if he was accepted, it would mean leaving baseball to join the military.

As frightened as he was at that possibility, Mickey knew it was his duty to help his country if he could. He showed up for his examination and did what he could to prove he was physically able. Amazingly, the injury that had once seemed likely to keep him from baseball allowed him to continue playing. The draft board classified Mickey as 4-F because of his osteomyelitis, a condition that could never be cured and therefore could recur at any point. A 4-F classification meant that Mickey was exempt from the military due to a physical limitation.

Mickey was thrilled to be free and clear to return to spring training in 1950. He was no longer as nervous about leaving his family for life on the road with a new baseball team and looked forward to the chance to improve on the previous year's stats. His confidence was growing, and it showed. Mickey could run the fastest sprint at spring training camp, a huge skill for a baseball player since part of the game involves making it to a base before the ball does. On only the fourth day, he slammed home

❝ *[1950 spring training] was one of the most fun times I ever had. Not a care in the world from the middle of March until mid-April.*❞

—MICKEY MANTLE

runs from both sides of the plate during an intrasquad game. Mickey was bumped up to the Yankees' Class AAA Kansas City team for the rest of spring training, and he held his own in practice with New York's top minor-league squad.

When spring training wrapped up, Mickey was rewarded for his impressive playing by a slight promotion from his Independence, Kansas, Class D team to a Class C team in Joplin, Missouri, the Joplin Miners. Mickey knew it was time to get down to business. If he wanted to make it to "The Show," as the major leagues are called, then he had to prove he deserved it this year in Joplin.

Chapter Four

The Waiting Game

Certain teams just have a special spark, something about the combination of players in that particular time that makes the team blaze past everyone in their path. The 1950 Joplin Miners quickly became one of those teams. By the middle of the season, they led the pack by more than twenty games.

A restaurant in Joplin started a steak giveaway in 1950, handing out a free piece of meat for every home run the Miners hit. Thanks to Mickey, a lot of people ate for free!

And it was clear to everyone who watched them play that there was one giant reason for the Miners' success: Mickey Mantle.

Mickey had truly come into his own, as if his body somehow understood that it needed to happen *now*. "The year before he [weighed] 160, 165," remembers Steve Kraly, one of Mickey's roommates that season. "At Joplin he was all filled out . . . and instead of hitting an occasional ball over the left-field wall, he was hitting these things over the light towers."

Still, Mickey didn't let up on himself to keep improving, and neither did his father. Mutt attended many of the Miners' home games, and even at the height of Mickey's success, his father continued to remind him of what he could be doing better. Maybe it was because he knew Mutt was in the stands watching that by the end of the Miners' season, Mickey had stacked up some amazing stats. He led the Western Association in hits with 199, and his 141 runs and 326 total bases also nabbed him the top spots in those categories. Capping it off was his league batting title with a solid .383 average. Mickey was just warming up. He was ready to show the minor leagues who they were dealing with!

Mickey achieved a staggering .402 batting average during the Yankees' 1951 preseason exhibition games.

But it wasn't just the folks in the minors who took notice. Mickey's stellar playing that season caught the eye of the New York Yankees themselves. When the Joplin team's season wrapped up, Mickey got the news he and his dad had been dying to hear. He was joining the Yankees for their final two-week road trip in September!

Mickey arrived at Sportsman's Park in St. Louis on Sunday, September 17, 1950, torn between incredible excitement and sheer terror. He couldn't believe he was actually going to be in the same locker room as the major leaguers he admired so much, including slugger Joe DiMaggio himself! Mickey was so intimidated by all these Yankee greats that he barely spoke a word to any of them. Luckily another rookie, Bill "Moose" Skowron, befriended Mickey. The two were roommates during the road trip, and they continued to spend time together when the team came back to New York for the last weeks of the season. "We didn't have much pocket money, so we'd usually go eat pizza somewhere," Skowron said. "'Cause I liked pizza and Mickey had never even heard of it before."

New York was full of surprises and adventures for the eighteen-year-old boy from the Midwest who'd never heard of pizza. "We'd get lost on the subways sometimes," Skowron said. "We'd never know where we'd wind up, only that sooner or later we'd find our way back." As new and overwhelming as life in the Big Apple was for Mickey, once he'd had a taste, he knew he wanted to come back for more.

After watching Mickey hit a particularly powerful homer, the equipment manager for the 1950 Joplin Miners told Mickey that it was the longest one he'd seen since witnessing Babe Ruth hit the ball out of Sportsman's Park during the 1928 World Series.

Mickey traveled home for the winter, where Mutt proudly told anyone who would listen that his son had worn a real Yankees uniform and actually knew Joe DiMaggio! Mickey enjoyed the time with his family and also with his hometown sweetheart, Merlyn Johnson. Mickey had met Merlyn the previous autumn, and it hadn't taken long for the two to fall in love. In fact, they'd actually met on a triple date where they *weren't* matched up with each other. When Mickey tried for a second date with the girl he'd gone out with, he wasn't too disappointed to hear she was busy. That meant he could call up Merlyn, the pretty brunette he'd had his eyes on the whole night anyway. Even though Mickey had been away playing baseball for many months, the connection with Merlyn had lasted. They picked up right where they had left off when he was back in Commerce.

But as much as he enjoyed spending time with the people he loved, where Mickey really wanted to be was with the New York Yankees. Would this be the year he would officially join the major-league roster?

In 1951 the Yankees held their spring training in Phoenix, Arizona, having traded their usual Florida spot with the New York Giants. Yankees manager Casey Stengel, in his third season with the team, was especially eager for the early spring instructional camp, held for Yankee players who weren't yet members of the major-league squad itself. Stengel was hoping to get a good look at the player he'd been hearing more and more about: Mickey Mantle. But when the camp got going, Mickey was nowhere to be seen. Where was he?

It turned out that Mickey was still in Commerce, patiently waiting for a plane or bus ticket to Arizona. The Mantles were still too poor to afford a phone in their house, and Mickey couldn't afford the travel costs on his own. Finally Tom Greenwade showed up in Commerce to personally hand over Mickey's train ticket to Phoenix.

Mickey may have gotten a late start at the instructional camp, but he quickly became the star of all the rookies there. Mickey was so fast in the races against other players that Stengel wondered whether he'd gotten a head start or the other guys had started late. When they timed Mickey's run from home plate to first base, his three-second sprint even beat any major leaguer's time.

❝ *He just did everything you'd ever want to see on a ball field. The home runs were only part of it. Casey [Stengel] said one time that the kid runs so fast he doesn't even bend the grass when he steps on it.* ❞

—TEAMMATE JOHNNY HOPP

One problem remained. Mickey wasn't a terribly impressive shortstop. In Independence and Joplin, he'd continued in the position he'd played since high school, but Casey Stengel felt it was time to make a change. He knew that the Yankees' general manager, George Weiss, thought Mickey needed another season or two before he would be major-league material. Stengel disagreed. He thought the time was ripe for bringing Mickey to New York and the key to making it happen was giving the player a new position that would maximize his strengths.

Eventually Stengel decided that this position was right field, since left field was a little too tough for a rookie and center field was still owned by DiMaggio. The timing was perfect. Long-running Yankee right fielder Tommy Henrich had just retired and was happy to work one-on-one with Mickey at the camp, training him to take over his old job. "He was a nice kid, very quiet, did everything that was ever asked of him—very, very dedicated," Henrich later said. Yeah, yeah, nice and dedicated—but could he *play?* "There was raw potential, but a lotta guys come up to the big leagues with potential," Henrich explained. As he kept watching . . . "I started seeing he was doing it right. He was perfect," Henrich admits.

Henrich wasn't the only one who agreed with Stengel that Mickey was headed for greatness. Once regular spring training got under way, Mickey was hotter than hot. Sportswriters instantly zeroed in on Mickey as the guy to watch, writing headlines about his power and speed. "He actually got the attention of opponents," said teammate Tommy Byrne. "You could see them all come forward in the dugout to watch him when he came up, even in batting practice, just to watch his swings."

One game in particular stands out in the minds of players who were there at the University of Southern California (USC) stadium on March 26, 1951. Mickey hit a single, a triple, and two

Mickey was clocked running the bases in just *thirteen seconds,* but Casey Stengel repeated the test several more times, convinced his watch had to be broken.

home runs that day. One of his homers left the ballpark, soared over an adjoining football field, and finally landed about 650 feet away from home plate. "It was hit so far it was like it wasn't real," said USC coach Rod Dedeaux. "It was a superhuman feat."

Despite the growing frenzy around Mickey and his "superhuman" abilities, he was far from convinced that joining the Yankee roster was a sure thing. Mickey had no clue that Casey Stengel was already certain Mickey would be the breakout star who would give him everything he needed to turn his team into a dynasty. When Mickey's friend Nick Ferguson called him and pretended to be the general manager from a Class AA team in Beaumont, Texas, asking him to report for the season, Mickey politely agreed, disappointed but not surprised.

After Nick started laughing and let Mickey in on the joke, Mickey was relieved but still afraid to get his hopes up. He could barely breathe when Casey Stengel brought him to George Weiss's car on the train ride to Washington, D.C., for the conversation that would give him his answer. Was he or wasn't he?

Soon the waiting was over. Stengel had convinced Weiss that Mickey was ready. Mickey was going to become a full-fledged New York Yankee!

Chapter Five

Too Much, Too Soon

Just when Mickey was sure that his dream of being a Yankee was finally coming true, he faced one last obstacle—the Oklahoma draft board. Even though Mickey had already failed one examination, his name was in the papers and the public wanted to know why this fit rookie baseball star couldn't fight for the military. By 1951 America was in the middle of the Korean War, and it seemed more important than ever that every strong young man join in the effort. Mickey went

---

66 *The kid doesn't run—he flies.* 99

—CASEY STENGEL

---

through his second physical exam, but the answer was still the same. As excellent as Mickey's current condition was, he had a chronic problem that was on the list of diseases disqualifying men for military service no matter what.

What a relief!

Still, Mickey could barely register the excitement of being named to the New York Yankees squad before the fear hit him of just how major this was—after all, he was in the *major* leagues! What would everyone think if he didn't prove he deserved the spot? What would his father think?

The pressure was as high as it could get, and for a nineteen-year-old boy coming to New York City from Oklahoma, that was pretty high! Mickey knew that Casey Stengel had boasted to reporters that his pet project, Mickey Mantle, was "Babe Ruth,

FOUR-SEWER MAN

One day during his early months in New York, Mickey joined a pickup stickball game at the corner of 162nd Street and Sheridan Avenue near his hotel. "Back then, you'd measure a guy by how many sewers he could hit the ball," says one of the former stickball regulars, Stephen Swid. "A really big hitter would be a three-sewer guy." After Mickey's visit, "the news spread all over the neighborhood and then throughout the Bronx: Mickey Mantle was a four-sewer man!"

Lou Gehrig, and Joe DiMaggio all rolled into one." Mickey had even been assigned a number 6 uniform, following directly after his predecessors—Ruth had worn number 3 and Gehrig number 4, and DiMaggio wore number 5. The rumblings were growing louder that hopes were pinned on Mickey to literally replace DiMaggio in his center-field spot since the famous player announced 1951 would be his last year as a Yankee. The fans— and slugger DiMaggio himself—would be waiting to see if Mickey deserved the sky-high expectations he was walking into.

The Yankees began the 1951 season at home in the legendary "house that Ruth built"—Yankee Stadium in the Bronx. They faced the Boston Red Sox, led by star Ted Williams.

Mickey was overcome by emotion at the reality of what was happening. But not so overcome that he couldn't help his team to a 5–0 victory! Mickey scored a hit on his third at bat after a quick conference with his idol DiMaggio. The hit drove home a runner on third base, giving Mickey the confidence to score a run of his own later in the game. The next day, he drove in two more runs, and the Yankees had another win. Major-league baseball was turning out to be a whole lot of fun!

For Mickey, none of his achievements were quite enough until he'd accomplished a major-league home run. His first major-league homer came on May 1 in Chicago. Another followed four days later in good old St. Louis. Even the skeptics

Ted Williams was a personal hero of Mickey's. After seeing Williams play in 1950, Mickey said, "I became convinced he was the greatest hitter I'd ever seen."

who'd wondered if Mickey was still too young and too green to fulfill Stengel's predictions were starting to waver. Maybe this kid *did* have what it took to be a baseball sensation.

Or did he?

By the end of June, the excitement and pressure of the season seemed to be taking a toll. Mickey's batting average had slid from near .320 in May to the .260s. He was striking out far too often, and with each strikeout the frustration built, making it harder to get back on track. The boos from fans who were loyal to DiMaggio and resentful of his supposed successor didn't help. Mickey had extra trouble earning support from the New York fans because he was naturally shy, which sometimes looked more like aloofness. He always tried to keep his head down as he ran the bases on a home run instead of tipping his hat to the fans as most players did. For Mickey, keeping his head down was a sign of respect for the pitcher. The fans thought Mickey didn't like them when he was playing well, so they weren't about to support him when he began having trouble.

Soon it became impossible to deny that Mickey was in a bona fide slump, every ballplayer's nightmare. Slumps are very common for rookies, but Mickey's was all the more noticed because he'd been given so much attention at the start of the season. And unfortunately, his slump happened to take place at the same time that his teammates were also struggling. Yankees management was starting to squirm as they saw their team slip out of first place. By mid-July the Yanks were all the way down to third, only one game ahead of the fourth-place Cleveland Indians. It was time for a serious intervention, and the decision was reached to bring on a new pitcher to revitalize the team. But adding one player to the roster meant subtracting another, and Mickey felt his heart fall when he was called to Casey Stengel's office for a "talk."

"This is gonna hurt me more than you," Stengel told Mickey, with tears in his eyes. The manager may have truly felt torn, but there wasn't much of a chance that he was as crushed as Mickey after delivering the news Mickey had been dreading— he was being sent back down to the minors.

Stengel assured his protégé that the move was temporary and that as soon as Mickey started hitting again, he'd be right back up there in the Bronx. Besides, they were sending Mickey to the Kansas City Blues, a AAA minor-league team just one step down from the majors. To Mickey, though, this was worse than if he'd spent the whole season in the minor leagues with the lower-ranked Class AA Beaumont team, still waiting for his shot at the big leagues. "I had been a Yankee, and now I was nothing," Mickey explained. "The same newspapers that had billed me as a superstar in April were now saying I was through."

Mickey's confidence was shattered. He arrived in Kansas City with all the strength sapped out of him. Meanwhile his new teammates didn't exactly welcome him with open arms. These guys were working hard to get where Mickey had already been, and they had never seen *their* names in major newspaper headlines. Everyone knew that if Mickey Mantle was in the minors again, it was only to get him fixed up and sent back to New York. Everyone knew, that is, except for Mickey. He was still convinced that he was going nowhere.

It soon became clear that playing for Kansas City wasn't going to pull him out of his slump. In fact, things were only getting worse. In his very first at bat, Mickey actually managed to get a bunt, and he felt a spark of encouragement. Then his coach, George Selkirk, barked at him that he wasn't there to bunt. "You're here to get some hits and get your confidence back," Selkirk reminded him.

The reprimand was the last straw, and from that moment on, Mickey couldn't buy a hit. His teammates were resentful, his coach was frustrated, and the angry letters from fans who still didn't understand his 4-F status kept pouring in. So Mickey turned to the one person who had always been there when he needed him, the reason he had made it as far as he did.

Mutt Mantle had barely heard his son's voice on the telephone when he hung up and started the five-hour car trip from Commerce to Kansas City. When he arrived, he realized things were even worse than he'd thought.

"I'll never make it," Mickey told his father. "I think I'll quit and go home with you."

Mickey held his breath as he waited for Mutt's response. All he wanted was for his dad to put his arms around him and agree that the Yankees just weren't giving Mickey a fair shot and to reassure him that things would get better.

Mutt fixed his son with a steady gaze and coolly informed him that perhaps Mickey was right. Perhaps he belonged back in Commerce, working in the mines alongside him. His final statement ripped right through Mickey, reaching him the way nothing else had. "I thought I raised a man, not a coward!"

Hearing the disappointment that filled his father's voice was the last thing in the world Mickey wanted. But it was, as he would later realize, exactly what he needed.

That very evening Mickey blasted out of his slump with two home runs while his father watched from the stands. Suddenly he was back, igniting the Kansas City Blues and bringing the team to the brink of the American Association Championship.

In Mickey's forty-one games with the Kansas City Blues, he slugged eleven home runs, fifty RBIs, three triples, and nine doubles.

Unfortunately for the Kansas City fans, the Yankees were watching, and they wanted Mickey back. The Yanks did have to wait in line behind the U.S. government. Mickey went through yet another physical exam to confirm his draft-exempt status before arriving in New York at the end of the summer. Soon it was official—Mickey was a Yankee again!

This time around Mickey was assigned number 7, and the number *switch* seemed to be just the trick for this famous switch-hitter. One day after rejoining the Yankees, Mickey whammed a home run against the Cleveland Indians, helping New York to a 7–3 victory. Mickey and the Yankees continued their strong run and that fall clinched the team's third-straight American League pennant.

Next up was the World Series, a true fantasy for Mickey. He was especially excited that Mutt was making the trip to New York to watch him and his team take on their hometown rival, the New York Giants. Mickey was determined to make his dad proud.

Fans across the country eagerly tuned in to the series. Not only was this the last World Series for star player Joe DiMaggio, but it was also a face-off between New York's two famous rookies—Mickey for the Yankees and Willie Mays for the Giants. Everyone knew this was going to be a hot matchup.

Mickey actually learned he was in the starting line-up for the 1951 World Series when he spotted the information on the sports page of a New York newspaper!

Mickey certainly felt the pressure, especially when Casey Stengel took him aside to warn him that DiMaggio's heel was hurting—Stengel worried that he couldn't cover center field as well as he once had. Casey asked Mickey to keep that in mind and extend his reach as far into right-center field as he could. The extra load Mickey felt he had to carry was probably part of the reason he didn't get a single hit as the Giants nabbed the first game, 5–1. Game two was a different story, and Mickey managed a drag bunt single in the third inning that eventually led to a run. He'd done it! He'd scored a run for his team in the WORLD SERIES.

❝They ought to create a new league for that guy.❞
—CHICAGO WHITE SOX PITCHER JACK HARSHMAN

Mickey was so ecstatic, he didn't think anything could ruin his mood. When Willie Mays himself came to bat in the sixth inning, Mickey took a few steps toward DiMaggio's center-field territory, remembering what Casey Stengel had told him. Sure enough, Mays hit the ball directly into right-center field. Mickey didn't hesitate. He ran for the ball, convinced DiMaggio wouldn't make it in time on his older legs. Just as Mickey was almost there, he heard the Yankee slugger call out, "I've got it." Mickey knew the way things worked. When a player like DiMaggio called it, you let him have the ball. He was so terrified of colliding with the nation's baseball hero that he stopped short, throwing on the brakes from his full-speed sprint. And then something went wrong. Very, very wrong.

When Mickey stopped, his spike caught on a drain hole in the grass. His right knee caved under him, and Mickey went down in a second. The crack his knee made as it broke was so loud that DiMaggio later said he thought Mickey had been shot. The injury, Mickey claimed, was so intense that he might as well have been shot. Mickey lay on the ground, sobbing. DiMaggio, confused at first, reassured Mickey that he'd caught the ball. But it soon became clear that Mickey's tears had nothing to do with his worries about the game and everything to do with the excruciating pain in his leg.

Sadly, as terrifying as that moment was, Mickey was about to confront something even worse—he was about to hear the most difficult news of his life.

Chapter | Six

Turning Point

Mickey had suffered injuries before, but it didn't take long for him to realize that the blow to his knee during the World Series game was like nothing he'd ever experienced. Mutt, himself concerned, brought his son to Lenox Hill Hospital. As they emerged from the taxi, Mickey leaned on Mutt for support, and suddenly Mutt collapsed to the ground.

"I couldn't understand it," Mickey said later. "He was a very strong man, and I didn't think anything at all about putting my weight on him that way." But Mutt had been losing his strength for a while before then, as Mickey would come to realize when he really thought about it. His dad had been much thinner the last few visits they'd shared, but Mickey hadn't noticed.

The Mantle men were admitted to the hospital and given beds right next to each other. Mickey was soon told that he would need surgery to repair the damage to his knee. But Mutt's diagnosis was far more serious. He had advanced Hodgkin's disease, the same illness that had already killed Charlie Mantle and two of Mutt's brothers. The disease was beginning to seem like a family curse.

Mickey, only nineteen, faced losing his father, the most important person in the world to him. No one knew better than Mickey that Mutt had molded him into the skilled baseball player he was becoming. It was a devastating blow, and one that Mickey admits changed his life forever.

Mickey and Mutt watched the Yankees go on to win the World Series on TV from their hospital beds, then returned together to Commerce for the winter. Mickey devoted himself entirely to making his father happy, even while clinging to the hope that a cure would emerge for his condition. Happily, winning the World Series meant the Yankees players each received bonus checks, and Mickey used his to buy a new home for his family. One of Mutt's remaining dreams for Mickey was that he marry his high school sweetheart, Merlyn. Mickey and Merlyn still shared a strong connection, even though Mickey had become involved in other relationships since moving to New York. Mickey cared for Merlyn, and he believed in his father's ability to know what was best for him. So on December 23, 1951, Mickey and Merlyn married in a very small ceremony at her parents' home.

Soon it was time for Mickey to leave for spring training, as hard as it was to part from his father. And he didn't have an easy road waiting for him with the Yankees, either. Mickey had figured that recovering from the knee injury would be similar to how it had been with the osteomyelitis flare-up—a quick progression to the same level of fitness he was accustomed to. "I thought the muscles would automatically come back, good as ever," he explained. "I was twenty years old, and I thought I was a superman." He was so convinced of this that he disregarded the team doctor's prescribed rehabilitation exercises, instead spending his time off resting and trying to cope with his fear of losing his father.

"I *always loved the game, but when my legs weren't hurting, it was a lot easier to love.***"**

—Mickey Mantle

But the muscles didn't automatically come back, and the Yankees' management was extremely disappointed to watch Mickey struggle to run during spring training. DiMaggio had retired, and Casey Stengel had intended to move Mickey to the vacant center-field position, but it clearly wasn't going to happen right away.

As he practiced, however, Mickey's speed did continue to pick up. He was also adjusting to life in New York, becoming more comfortable in the city that had initially overwhelmed him. He built friendships with some of his teammates, especially Billy Martin, who became like a big brother to him. Merlyn had also come along with Mickey for their first baseball season as a married couple, and the two spent a lot of time with Martin and his wife, Lois.

But Mickey's growing happiness in New York was shattered on May 6, 1952, when he received the phone call that he'd been dreading—his father had died. Mutt hadn't allowed his wife or children to know just how sick and close to the end he was, afraid to interfere with Mickey's concentration on the field. The shock and horror of the news left Mickey so raw that he couldn't share his grief with anyone, not even his new wife. He traveled home for the funeral alone, leaving Merlyn in New York.

As Mickey stood over his father's grave, he reeled from his death, haunted and overcome at the idea of never having Mutt there to watch another game he played. He was filled with regret for everything that had gone unsaid. "[I had] so many chances . . . to let him know how much I loved him—and I never said it, not once," Mickey recalled.

Mickey had always expressed his feelings for his father through his passion for baseball. After Mutt was gone, Mickey had all the love in the world to give him and no place to put it—except on the baseball field. He returned to New York and threw himself into the game. At first his playing was shaky. But on May 20, Stengel finally moved him to center field. By the end of the season, his stats were on the rise. The Yankees took the American League pennant and went on to face the Brooklyn Dodgers in the World Series.

In 1952 Philadelphia A's pitcher Al Benton became the only pitcher to go up against both Babe Ruth—whom Benton had faced during his rookie year with the Boston Red Sox in 1934—and Mickey Mantle. And Benton had an extra claim to fame, boasting that neither of the power hitters got a home run off of him!

It was time for Mickey to stare down his demons from the previous year's World Series, which had been full of heartbreak. Only he didn't just stare them down, he kicked them to pieces! Mickey had a phenomenal series, hitting .345 and slamming his first postseason home runs, including a game-winning homer in the sixth game and one in game seven that assured the Yankees of their 4–2 win and the championship.

The next season was a rockier one for Mickey as he watched his average fall below .300 and suffered another frustrating knee injury that kept him on the bench for more than thirty games. But the year certainly had its share of high notes. On April 12, 1953, Mickey stepped up to the plate at an exhibition game against the Brooklyn Dodgers at Ebbets Field and faced a happy surprise. The announcer followed his introduction for player number 7 with the words, "Mickey doesn't know it yet, but he just became the father of an eight-pound, twelve-ounce baby boy!"

Merlyn had stayed behind in Oklahoma to finish her pregnancy and to have her family's help once the baby was born. Mickey was thrilled to hear about his son, soon named Mickey Jr., and couldn't wait to meet him. But he would have to wait for over a month since the Yankees weren't about to lose their ace hitter during the crucial first part of the season. And in fact, just five days later came Mickey's awe-inspiring home run at Griffith Stadium, the Washington Wallop that set a whole new standard for the tape-measure homer.

Mickey had three nicknames: "The Mick," "The Commerce Comet," and "The Switcher."

With its ups and downs, the 1953 season ended on a definite "up" for Mickey. The Yankees made it back to the World Series, and this one was extra-special because it was actually the fiftieth anniversary of the first World Series back in 1903. To commemorate the occasion, the first pitch was thrown out by baseball great Cy Young, and Mickey was honored to be in the stadium with him. If he'd needed that extra bit of motivation to give what he could to his team, seeing Cy Young on the field sure did it!

The Yankees faced a rematch in the series against the Brooklyn Dodgers. The Dodgers were fresh off an especially strong season, nicknamed the "Boys of Summer" for their stunning display of talent, and they were hungry to take the title from their uptown rival. Mickey knew it was up to him to stop them.

First he hit a home run in the eighth inning of game two that also drove in another runner, giving the Yankees a 4–2 lead and the win. The Yankees led the series 2–0. The Dodgers weren't giving up easily, however, and they fought back in games three and four, evening out the playing field.

Mickey and his buddy Billy Martin came on strong together in game five. Both contributed to a thrilling 11–7 victory for the Yankees. But it was Mickey's star play in that game that sent the stadium into a frenzy. When he came to bat in the third inning,

Mickey faced the situation that can be every baseball player's greatest dream or worst nightmare—bases loaded, two out. It's a chance to score big or just let everyone down. The Dodgers had carefully selected a right-handed pitcher, forcing Mickey to hit from the left side, his weaker stance. However, all the strategy in the world couldn't save the Dodgers when Mickey's bat connected with the pitch and sent the ball soaring! Mickey became the fourth player ever to hit a grand slam home run during a World Series game. The Dodgers never recovered, and the Yankees went on to snap up the title once again.

What was that again about Mickey's *weaker* side?

Mickey was as relieved as he was excited about the big play in game five. He felt more secure about his spot on the Yankees, and the well-earned paycheck supported his widowed mother and his own growing family.

Mickey's running speed was noticed across the major leagues. His idol Ted Williams, a pilot in the Korean War, told the story of landing and miraculously escaping a fighter plane that was on fire and about to explode. Williams said, "I got outta there, and I must have been running as fast as Mantle."

If Mickey was worried that his job wasn't safe, his performance in 1954 took care of that. He broke the 100 mark for RBIs for the first time and led the Yankees with twenty-seven home runs. Still, the strong year for Mickey didn't translate into a strong enough year for his team, which lost to Cleveland for the American League pennant and the chance to compete in the World Series. It was the first year in Mickey's professional career that he hadn't made it to the championship series, and he was determined to do everything he could to make it his last.

❝*[Baseball] wasn't a game to me . . . it was my job and my living and all I knew. Without it, I was going to be digging fence posts back in Commerce or carrying a pick down to the zinc mines.*❞

—MICKEY MANTLE

Chapter Seven

Crown Prince

The 1955 season got off to a great start for Mickey. On May 13, the Yankees hosted the Detroit Tigers in a home game, and Mickey single-handedly trounced the Tigers. Not only did he drive in each of the Yankees' five runs, he also marked the day with the only three-homer game of his professional career. He hit two home runs from the right side of the plate and one from the left.

Mickey was just warming up, and his stats continued to shoot up. But on September 16, Mickey felt a sharp pain in the back of his right thigh during a bunt attempt. It was an all too familiar disappointment—he had torn a muscle, and he'd have to settle for a thirty-seven-homer season. Even so, that number was enough to earn him the top spot in the league for home runs, a new accomplishment for Mickey. His final batting average for the regular season was .306.

Luckily Mickey's injury came late enough in the season that it didn't keep the Yankees from regaining their pennant title, to Mickey's relief. They were back in the World Series!

A World Series pitting the Yankees against the Dodgers was almost becoming a fall ritual. The Dodgers were coming off another ace season, having easily won the National League pennant. But the Dodgers' postseason was—literally—a whole different ball game. They just couldn't seem to come through when the world championship title was on the line. It looked like this year was going to be the same story as the Yankees took the first two games of the series, with 6–5 and 4–2 victories. Mickey watched his team win from the sidelines, his thigh injury still keeping him on the bench. After teammate Hank Bauer pulled a muscle in game two, however, Mickey joined his squad for game three, fighting off the pain.

BASEBALL BROTHERS

Mickey's twin brothers, Ray and Roy Mantle, came close to playing alongside him on the Yankees. In 1955 Ray and Roy attended the Yankees' spring training instructional camp and played well enough to be assigned spots on Class C minor-league teams. But after Roy injured a leg and Ray was drafted into the army, Mickey's dream of playing with his brothers was stopped short.

Mickey, wearing number 14, was a star guard for his Commerce High School basketball team.

The Mantle family in 1949. Back row *(left to right):* Ray, Roy, Barbara. Front row *(left to right):* Mutt, Lovell, Larry, Mickey

Mickey and Joe DiMaggio together at a 1951 training camp. It was the only year they played together.

Mickey in 1951, his first year with the Yankees

Showing off a strong batting stance

Batting right-handed against the Chicago White Sox on May 18, 1956, Mickey hit his fourteenth and fifteenth homers of the season—one from each side of the plate—at this game.

Taking a giant, left-handed swing

National Baseball Hall of Fame Library, Cooperstown, NY

Mickey with Casey Stengel, the manager he said had been almost like a father to him

Mickey slamming another one against the Cleveland Indians in 1967. It was his sixteenth year with the Yankees.

Casey Stengel stands between Mickey and Whitey Ford. Both players were inducted into baseball's Hall of Fame on August 12, 1974.

Even injured, Mickey knew how to make things happen on the field. He scored a home run in the second inning to give the Yankees one of their three runs. Unfortunately, it wasn't enough, and the Dodgers creamed them, 8–3. On a roll, the Dodgers tied up the series with another win in game four and then pulled ahead in game five, which Mickey was forced to sit out to give his sore leg a break. Uh-oh—one more Dodgers victory and the Yankees would be waving good-bye to the World Series title.

"All of a sudden, we had our backs to the wall and I was practically helpless," Mickey later recalled in one of his books, "but I was still confident we could win." After all, the sixth and seventh games were both on Yankee home turf.

Mickey was especially happy that his teammate Whitey Ford was pitching for the Yankees in game six. Mickey knew Ford was a top-notch pitcher. Ford came through in style, handing his team a clean 5–1 win to even the series at three games apiece, making this a fight to the finish.

The pressure was on for game seven. Whoever won would be the next world champion. Mickey was going out of his mind watching the action from the bench, wishing like crazy he could be out there helping his team. But he still believed they could do it without him. Even after the Dodgers scored two runs without any answer from the Yankees, Mickey kept the faith. And at the bottom of the sixth inning, it looked like the game was about to turn around. Billy Martin was on second, Gil McDougald was on first, and three strong hitters were in line to come up and finish the job, starting with clutch player Yogi Berra.

"This was our big chance and I was certain we would win the game right there, mainly because of Yog," Mickey wrote. Yogi didn't disappoint, connecting with the ball for a hard drive down the left-field line. Mickey watched the ball soar, letting out a sigh of relief. Then his breath caught from amazement at what he saw. Dodgers outfielder Sandy Amoros was racing at breakneck speed toward the ball, about to make what looked like an impossible catch. In seconds it became obvious that the catch was indeed possible—because Amoros made it. Mickey was stunned and later claimed that if Amoros hadn't been left-handed, his glove never would have been able to reach the ball.

The Yankees' chances for evening the score were blown. They never did manage a single run, and the final score of 2–0 gave the Brooklyn Dodgers their first World Series championship.

Knowing the Dodgers were a talented team that deserved the title softened the blow a little, but it was still hard for Mickey to deal with his first World Series loss. If he'd been inspired in 1955, it was nothing next to the fire he brought into the 1956 season. The buzz started up as early as spring training. "This is Mickey Mantle's year," wrote one reporter in the *Washington Post*. Mickey's idol Ted Williams strongly agreed, saying, "My guess is that he's now definitely headed for his peak."

It sure looked that way on opening day, with the Yankees in Washington, D.C., at Griffith Stadium, facing the Senators. Mickey came to bat in the first inning and immediately knocked off a home run that traveled 465 feet to clear the center-field fence. Before the day was over, Mickey had another homer, which also flew right past center field. It was a great start for Mickey, and the Yankees came along for the ride. They took first place in the league at the end of April with an 8–3 record for the month.

---

66 *No man in the history of baseball had as much power as Mickey Mantle.* 99

—YANKEE TEAMMATE BILLY MARTIN

Early in May, Mickey notched his ninth home run of the season in only his sixteenth game. He was on the fast track for a high-homer year. In fact, journalists checked the stats for Babe Ruth back in 1927, the year the Babe had set the record with an incredible sixty home runs. What they found only fed the excitement that surrounded Mickey. Babe hadn't had his ninth homer in 1927 until his twenty-ninth game! Was this it, finally? The year Babe Ruth's record would be smashed by whiz kid Mickey Mantle?

❝ *It just didn't seem possible that a ball could be hit that hard.* **❞**

—YANKEE HISTORIAN PETER GOLENBOCK ON THE POWER OF MICKEY'S NINETEENTH HOME RUN IN THE 1956 SEASON

Mickey certainly seemed unstoppable. His batting average was up to an amazing .446, and his team was racking up win after win. Mickey wasn't sure if he really had a shot at breaking the Babe's home run record, but he was starting to hope for something else—a Triple Crown for hitting, meaning that by season's end, he'd hold the top spot in the league for batting average, home runs, and RBIs. Only eleven players had ever achieved a Triple Crown before, and Mickey knew the goal wouldn't be easy, but the challenge made it all the more fun.

On Memorial Day, the Yankees had a doubleheader—two games in one day—against the Washington Senators at home in Yankee Stadium. Mickey came to bat in the fifth inning and racked up two balls and two strikes. Mickey slammed the next pitch as hard as he could. While a home run for Mickey Mantle was nothing new, he later described this homer as his best left-handed hit ever. The ball only just missed flying out of the top of the stadium—the closest any fair ball at Yankee Stadium had come until that moment.

By the All-Star break in early July, Mickey had a whopping twenty-nine home runs, one game ahead of Babe Ruth's pace, and the Yankees were fresh off a five-game winning streak. The wins continued after the break, and August wrapped up with a total of forty-seven home runs for Mickey. His chances of beating the Babe were looking better and better every day.

Mickey scored two home runs in only two of the twenty All-Star Games he played in—one in 1955 and the other in 1956.

Then, in the first week of September, Mickey suffered yet another injury, this time a pulled groin muscle. Once again his body was letting him down, standing in the way of an achievement he'd seemed primed for all season. Mickey's fiftieth home run didn't come until September 18, and the hope for breaking Babe Ruth's record faded fast.

Even scarier, Mickey's chance at the Triple Crown also began to slip through his grasp. Ted Williams breezed by him in the batting average race, and Mickey realized he had to come back—and fast. He shut out the pain from his injury, as he'd done for so much of his career, and forgot about Babe Ruth's record.

The Yankees had enjoyed such a strong season that they'd clinched the pennant race on September 18. All Mickey had to do was finish the season on a high note and prove to the world that he could be the kind of player Casey Stengel had said he was back in 1951.

On two legs, Mickey Mantle would have been the greatest ballplayer who ever lived.

—CHICAGO WHITE SOX PLAYER NELLIE FOX, REFERRING TO MICKEY'S BADLY INJURED LEG, WHICH WAS NEVER THE SAME AFTER THE 1951 WORLD SERIES FALL

First there was a home run title to win. Soon enough Mickey had done it, with a season total of fifty-two. Then he had to fight off Williams directly for the batting title during an exciting final series between the Yankees and Williams's Red Sox. Going into the series, Mickey had regained the lead, but his .354 average was still just four percentage points above that of Williams. Mickey gave everything he had to hold on, despite the ongoing problems from his muscle pull. In the end, Mickey came away with a strong .353 average, while Williams dropped down to .345. All Mickey had to do was wait for the final piece to fall into place—the RBI title.

Detroit's Al Kaline went into his final game with 126 RBIs, giving him a chance to tie or top Mickey's 130. After a close final game, Mickey was ecstatic to hear the final results. Kaline had added only two more RBIs, falling short of Mickey's record.

Mickey Mantle had just become the twelfth player ever to win the Triple Crown.

 Along with his Triple Crown, Mickey had the highest figures for both his own league and the National League in 1956, becoming the fourth player in history to accomplish that in a season.

Chapter Eight

Perfect Game

Winning the Triple Crown had been the most thrilling moment of Mickey's baseball career so far. His one regret was that his father couldn't be there with him. "Not a day went by that year . . . that I didn't think of him and wished he'd gotten to live long enough to see it," Mickey said. Finally winning his first Most Valuable Player award for the season was another bittersweet triumph. Mickey was extremely gratified to have the honor but wished he could have shared it with Mutt Mantle. Without Mutt, there would have been no Triple Crown.

In 1956 Mickey became only the second player in baseball history to win the MVP award with a unanimous vote.

Even with all of his personal glory, Mickey was a team player through and through, and he knew his joy wouldn't be complete without the Yankees regaining their World Series title as well. "My Triple Crown season would have meant nothing, it would have been a waste, unless we got the world championship back," he wrote.

EVERYBODY LOVES MICKEY

Mickey Mantle began to cross over from being a baseball star to a pop culture icon after his Triple Crown success. Before the World Series, the *Kraft Television Theater* aired "The Mickey Mantle Story," and Mickey sang along with singer Teresa Brewer when she recorded the song "I Love Mickey."

Mickey and the rest of the Yankees were especially happy to learn they'd be having a rematch of last year's World Series battle since the Dodgers had again won the National League pennant. The first two games were played in Brooklyn, giving the Dodgers a home-field edge. Could the Yankees psych out the team that had taken away their title the year before with rival fans surrounding them?

A home run from Mickey early in game one gave the Yankees a 2–0 lead to start, but Brooklyn caught up and then zoomed right past them. The final score was 6–3 in favor of the Dodgers. The Yankees began the second game of the series with an even wider lead, 6–0. Once again Brooklyn fought back, driving up the score. The teams continued to trade runs, but in the end the Dodgers beat the Yankees 13–8.

It was a tough blow for the Yankees, but the good news was that they'd be following the two losses with three games back on their turf in the Bronx. "We knew these three games at home were crucial," Mickey recalled, "and we knew we had to sweep them." Anything less would have meant, at best, returning to Brooklyn with the challenge of winning both the sixth and seventh games on enemy territory.

This time it was the Dodgers who grabbed the first lead, with a run in the top of the second inning. The Yankees tied things up in the bottom half, and then Brooklyn scored again at the top of the sixth. The Yankees came right back when they were at bat, pulling ahead to a 4–2 lead. The Dodgers squeezed out one more run, but so did the Yankees, who finished with their first win of the series, 5–3.

The Yankees were back in the game!

Energized, Mickey threw in several important contributions to game four. He had a run in the fourth inning and then his next homer of the series in the sixth. With Mickey's help, the Yankees came away with a 6–2 victory and tied the World Series.

Game five of the series took place on Monday, October 8, a day Mickey described as "a beautiful autumn day in New York . . . a perfect day for baseball." There definitely seemed to be some magic in the air, and Mickey was about to experience a game he would later describe as "probably the biggest game I ever played in."

Every baseball pitcher has a fantasy of throwing a perfect game, a game in which the opposing team isn't able to get a single player on base. In a perfect game, a pitcher has to pitch flawlessly, and his team must play equally well. If a batter manages to make contact with the ball, the fielders have to catch it right away or the perfect game will be ruined. Pitching for the Yankees that day was Don Larsen, a solid player but hardly the ace (top pitcher) on the team.

"Right from the start, Larsen looked like he had his good stuff," Mickey remembered of the beginning of game five. But Larsen wasn't the only one throwing well that day. The Dodgers' pitcher, Sal Maglie, matched Larsen's perfection through three innings. Was this World Series crowd about to witness a perfect game pitched by *both* pitchers? Mickey knew he had to make sure that only Larsen got the distinction and the win.

It didn't take long to achieve this goal. In the bottom of the fourth inning, Mickey knocked out a game-breaking homer. Maglie's perfect game had been nipped in the bud, and the Yankees had a 1–0 lead.

As the game went on without any Dodger base runners, the heat turned up for the Yankees. This wasn't just about winning a game anymore or even about putting them one step closer to a world championship. The team was on the brink of having the first perfect game in the history of the World Series.

Every time a Brooklyn player came to bat, Mickey tensed his whole body, ready to run his heart out for the ball if the player connected. Then in the fifth inning, Dodger first baseman Gil Hodges hit a fastball off of Larsen, sending the ball soaring into left-center field. Mickey's heart jumped into his throat. "I just put my head down and took off as fast I could," he said. Mickey raced at full speed, catching up with the ball as it started its descent toward the grass. He nearly passed out from relief as he felt the ball "plop" into his glove, later calling that moment the best catch he'd ever made. Don Larsen thought so, too. After Mickey's heroic play, Larsen continued with his inspired pitching to achieve the ultimate, a *perfect* World Series game.

For all the credit given to Don Larsen, many fans and sportswriters felt it was another Yankee who should share in the glory of that game. "There would have been no perfect game for

Larsen without what Mantle did to catch Hodges's line drive," wrote one journalist. "That ball was certain to fall in until a flying Mantle reached the scene from nowhere." Larsen was the first to agree, saying, "I'll never forget the catch [Mickey] made to save the game."

Many doubted the Dodgers had what it took to come back from such a huge defeat, but the Brooklyn squad was tough. They managed to take game six from the Yankees in overtime after nine scoreless innings, with a score of just 1–0.

There was no way the Yankees would let go of this series easily, not after making history in game five. Coming together on a few excellent team plays, they knocked the Dodgers clean out of their own home stadium in game seven, finishing them off with a 9–0 victory. Mickey's Triple Crown year had ended with yet another world championship win!

&&*[1956 was] a year I'll never forget. My favorite summer.*&&
—MICKEY MANTLE

Going into the 1957 season, Mickey knew he had a real challenge facing him to match what he'd done the year before, but he still gave it his best shot. By the end of the year, he had his best batting average ever—.365. His other stats were down from the previous season, and Ted Williams came away with the batting title this go-around. Yet Mickey was named the league's MVP for the second time in a row.

Mickey and Ted Williams both shot through the .500 on-base percentage in 1957 and were the last players to do so until Barry Bonds in 2001.

The Yankees made it back to the World Series, this time facing the Milwaukee Braves. The series was a tug-of-war, stretching to seven games, but it was the Braves who came out on top in the final hour.

As always, Mickey and his teammates rebounded from the loss in style, taking the league by storm in 1958. The Yankees charged ahead to an early lead and eventually snagged the pennant by a good ten games over the second-place team, the Chicago White Sox. Mickey finished the season with a .304 average and led the league with forty-two home runs. An injury to his right shoulder slowed him down a little. In fact, Mickey realized he hadn't made it through a single season healthy, and he often wondered what he could have done if he had.

The Yankees had themselves another rematch World Series in 1958 against the Milwaukee Braves. It looked like history was about to repeat itself when the Braves went up three games to one, a deficit no team had ever been able to overcome in past World Series. But the Yankees were all about making history, and they came back from behind to reclaim their world championship title.

&& *When Little League uniforms were handed out every spring, the only real fight was for number 7; everything else was an afterthought.* &&

—Texas columnist Mike Leggett

Mickey had been playing with the Yankees for eight years and was twenty-seven years old. Sometimes he couldn't believe how much he'd already accomplished, but most of the time his focus was on doing it all over again the following year, only better. Mickey was so committed to his baseball career, in fact, that he didn't see much of his wife and growing family, who had moved to Dallas, Texas, in 1956. They wanted to be close to a large airport and to avoid the increased interruption of their personal lives that had been a problem in the small town of Commerce. Little Mickey Jr. had been joined by a brother, David, in December 1955. And when Mickey returned home from the

1958 season, he was just in time for the birth of his third son, Billy, in November. Fourth and last son Danny would come along in March 1960. At first Merlyn would bring the boys to rented homes in New Jersey during the baseball season so the family could stay together, but this disruption of their lives became increasingly hard as the boys grew older, and eventually they stayed behind in Texas. Mickey loved his sons very deeply but could never shake the idea that he still had a mission to fulfill on the baseball field in his father's memory. As long as he had it in him to be a great ballplayer, that was where his primary devotion lay.

All the devotion in the world couldn't help Mickey or his team during the 1959 season, however. The Yankees slid down the American League as the year wore on, briefly even occupying the dead last spot. They eventually finished in third place. Mickey's batting average dipped to .285, going below .300 for the first time since 1953. He'd never managed to fully escape the boos from fans that had trailed him since he first replaced Joe DiMaggio, but they had become harsher than ever as he floundered on the field. Mickey, along with the Yankees, was definitely in trouble—and it was time for some major changes if the team hoped to have a turnaround for 1960.

Chapter Nine

The M&M Boys

Part of baseball life is to see teammates you've played alongside for years suddenly traded to other teams. Overnight they become your opponents, while players who were once your opponents become your teammates. Mickey, who had formed especially strong attachments to other members of the Yankee squad, was always sad to see his friends leave. Billy Martin had gone to Kansas City, for example, and Mickey missed their friendship. But there was no denying the importance of the trade that brought Roger Maris to the Yankees in time for the 1960 season.

Maris had begun his major-league career with the Cleveland Indians, moving to the Kansas City A's in 1958. Like Mickey, Roger Maris had suffered a brutal injury during his rookie season. He'd broken three ribs on a headfirst slide for base, ruining his hopes for a Rookie of the Year award. Also like

Mickey, Roger Maris could hit homers—and lots of 'em.

With Mickey and Maris back-to-back in the batting lineup, the Yankees powered to a season total of 193 home runs, forty-three more than the closest runner-up team, Detroit. Close to half of those home runs came from Mickey and Roger alone, with Mickey hitting forty and Roger coming in just behind him at thirty-nine. Where Roger came out on top, however, was in the voting for that year's MVP award, which was the closest it had ever been.

> The Washington Senators gave Mickey more home runs than any other team—a career total of eighty.

Still, despite Mickey losing out on the official title, his popularity with fans had enjoyed a major upswing over the course of the season, due to the combination of his strong playing and his increased efforts to respond to the crowd. Mickey realized that acknowledging the fans let them feel they were sharing in the moment, a necessary part of the game.

And what a moment it was! The Yankees surged forward at the end of the season, ending on an exciting fifteen-game winning streak. It was time once again for the Yankees to go to the World Series. This year they'd play against the Pittsburgh Pirates, a team that didn't look that strong on paper.

Mickey entered the series confident that his team was in great shape and had what it took to beat the Pirates. Unfortunately, game one went to the Pirates, 6–4. But the Yankees were right back in it, winning game two 16–3 and game three 10–0. The shutout was courtesy of Whitey Ford's first pitching effort in the series. Mickey was glad to help, as always, and contributed two home runs in the second game and another in the third. Games four and five were disappointing losses, 3–2 and 5–2. Then Ford was back on the pitcher's mound for the sixth game and handed his team another shutout, this time a whopping 12–0!

It was down to game seven, and Mickey couldn't help being surprised that the series had lasted this long. But the real shock came when the Yankees suffered a crushing defeat, with a final score of 10–9, after the Pirates made their last run at the bottom of the ninth inning.

Mickey couldn't believe it. The Yankees had outscored the Pirates overall by a huge margin—55–27—and had also had ten homers to the Pirates' four. In fact, it was so clear that the Yankees were the better team that the winner of the series MVP award was actually a member of the *losing* team, Yankee Bobby Richardson!

"I was so disappointed," Mickey later wrote of the loss. "I cried on the plane ride home." Yankee fans and management were equally frustrated, and many shared Mickey's belief that a different pitching lineup from Casey Stengel—featuring Whitey Ford in more games—would have given the Yankees the championship. Yankee management decided to make a change. For the 1961 season, Stengel was out, and new manager Ralph Houk was in.

One of Houk's first acts as manager was to approach Mickey and ask him to act as a leader to the team. "It's your team," Houk told Mickey. Mickey took the words seriously, realizing that it was his place to reach out to the other players as a teammate and a friend and to set a good example of playing ball the way it was meant to be done.

❝Just from [Mickey] playing every day and never complaining, he was the leader. . . . When you knew the sort of pain he played with every day, never complaining, never asking out, he made everyone around him want to do better.❞

—Yankee teammate Johnny Blanchard

It turned out the other Yankees didn't need much help from Mickey in that area because the Yankees of 1961 were on fire!

Great pitching? Got it. Whitey Ford had his first twenty-win season, ending up with a 25–4 record. Great hitting? The team set a major-league record of 240 team home runs, on top of *another* record of six players hitting twenty or more homers. Great all-around playing? The Yankees won a remarkable 109 games out of the season's total of 162. Even with the Yankees playing great team ball, the real spotlight that summer was on the two players who seemed to be hitting home runs every time you turned around—Mickey Mantle and Roger Maris.

Mickey had a total of ten switch-hit homer games—games in which he hit homers from both sides of the plate.

By the end of June, Mickey and Roger were neck and neck, on the verge of breaking thirty home runs, and fans started to get excited. For the first time since 1956, it looked like Mickey had a real shot at breaking Babe Ruth's record of sixty home runs in a single season. And this time, he wasn't alone. He was locked in a thrilling home run derby with his own teammate!

Mickey had been here before, and he knew things could change. Yet the excitement was hard to avoid. It wasn't until

Mickey was being challenged that he finally won the unconditional support of the New York fans. Suddenly it was Mickey who was the "true" Yankee, while Roger Maris—who was as shy with reporters and fans as Mickey had once been—gained a reputation for being aloof and unfriendly.

Mickey's teammate Clete Boyer felt the problem for Mickey hadn't just been the public controversy of the 4-F draft exemption but also the incredibly high expectations Casey Stengel had built for Mickey. "Roger took the pressure off Mickey," Boyer said. "They never booed Mickey again. It became good guy–bad guy."

The press picked up on this idea, printing stories about Mickey and Roger having a hot rivalry on and off the field. Actually, the "M&M Boys," as they were soon nicknamed, were good friends who even lived together along with another Yankee, Bob Cerv. "Roger was as good a man and as good a ballplayer as there ever was," Mickey said in admiration of his teammate.

Mickey had always thrived on competition. Some of his best hitting stats had come from battling Ted Williams for season records. So he and Roger enjoyed the home run derby as a chance to push them both to excel. "I rooted for him and definitely rooted for myself," he wrote in one of his books. "Besides, with Roger hitting good it made me try harder."

It worked both ways. Mickey's extraordinary power helped Roger out, too, and not just because of the extra inspiration.

Early in the season Ralph Houk switched the batting order so that Mickey batted after Roger instead of the other way around. Mickey was moved to what was called the cleanup spot, the position reserved for the player who could be counted on to bat in any players on base. Roger Maris wasn't walked intentionally a single time in 1961 because opposing teams would never take the risk, knowing Mickey was next at bat. This meant Roger had better pitches to hit than Mickey did. Some say this development slanted the odds in his favor for the home run derby.

❝*I'll tell ya', and this is no knock on the Babe, they'd tell you that Ruth hit one here and hit one there, but with Mickey it was like he hit thirty from each side of the plate. There's nobody who will ever hit home runs the way he did, with the power and consistency.*❞

—YANKEE GENE WOODLING

The odds for both players took a hit in July when baseball commissioner Ford Frick—a good friend of Babe Ruth's—added a twist to the most-hyped race of baseball that year. Frick ruled that to break Babe's record, a player would have to hit more than sixty home runs within 154 games, the number of games that had been in the season when Babe was playing, versus the current 162 games. The pressure was more intense than ever—

Mickey and Roger had eight fewer games in which to score those sixty-one homers.

By early September, things looked good for *both* the M&M boys. Roger had fifty-six home runs and Mickey fifty-three. What fans couldn't see was the toll the stress took on the two players. Roger started losing patches of hair, and Mickey came down with a flu he just couldn't shake.

Noticing how run-down Mickey looked, a Yankee broadcaster recommended a doctor in New York who could "fix you right up." Mickey went to the doctor and received an injection, which was delivered directly into his hip. Within days the injection site was infected and bleeding badly. Mickey—used to playing through pain—made it through a couple more games and notched his fifty-fourth home run. But his leg got so bad that he was finally forced to go to the hospital for treatment. To clear away the infection, doctors had to cut a deep hole in Mickey's hip, and he was stuck watching the Yankees play from his hospital bed.

Mickey's quest for the record was over, but he rooted for his friend. The Yankees' 154th game was against Baltimore, and all eyes across the country were on Roger Maris. He scored his fifty-ninth homer that night but failed to rack up another two. Still, many fans weren't as concerned with the distinction Frick had made about how the score would go down in record books. They just wanted to see if Roger Maris could get sixty-one home runs in one season. Mickey cheered louder than anyone when Roger slugged his sixty-first homer on October 1, 1961.

❝The greatest thing I ever saw was Roger Maris breaking Babe Ruth's record.❞

—MICKEY MANTLE

"The only regret I have about it was that I wish I'd been healthy enough to give him a better run," Mickey admitted. It was truly the story of Mickey's life. How many times had he come so close to ultimate achievement and been held back by his own body's limits?

Of course, the other part of that story was Mickey's sheer determination to play again as soon as possible and even when he really wasn't fully recovered. The Yankees were back in the World Series that fall, facing the Cincinnati Reds. Mickey had his leg bandaged extensively so he could join his team for games three and four. "It was unbelievable this guy could walk, much less play," said teammate Johnny Blanchard, after catching sight of Mickey's infected hip in the clubhouse.

In game four, Mickey pushed it too far when he went all out to catch a ball and reopened the wound. He kept quiet about the pain, and no one knew anything was wrong until he came to bat. "He could barely stand," wrote journalist Jim Murray in the *Los Angeles Times*. "He hit one off the center-field fence but barely made first base like a guy crawling with an arrow in his back." Teammates realized in horror that Mickey's pants were covered in blood, and Mickey was taken out of the game and sent right back to the hospital. Still, his brave contributions helped the Yankees win the game after a pinch runner came in to finish the run he'd started. After game five, the series and championship title belonged to the Yankees once more.

Despite being frustrated yet again by an injury, Mickey had enjoyed another brilliant season. He couldn't wait for the following year!

❝*Give me the Mick in the clutch anytime.***❞**

—RALPH HOUK

Chapter Ten

Hall of Famer

Although it couldn't quite compare to the glorious summer of 1961, the 1962 season did have its high moments for Mickey. An injury in May and then others to follow kept him out of a total of thirty-nine games, but he still hit thirty home runs in the 123 games in which he did play. Capping off the year was Mickey's third MVP honor, awarded to him despite the fact that he hadn't led the league in home runs, batting average, or runs batted in. "What did he lead the league in?" said Yankee publicist Jackie Ferell in response. "He led the league in manhood, that's what."

> In 1962, Mickey's third and final MVP year, the Yankees were 75–42 with him in the starting lineup and 21–24 without him there.

The season ended just the way Mickey liked it, with a pennant and another World Series win. Mickey's long list of accomplishments finally convinced the team's management to up his salary to $100,000 for the next year, making him the first Yankee since Joe DiMaggio to earn that much.

Mickey started out the 1963 season proving he deserved every penny, slugging a power home run on May 22. June brought another major injury, this time a broken foot, and Mickey still wasn't very good at sticking to his rehabilitation schedule.

It had also been a long time since Mickey had eaten his very first slice of pizza in New York. Over the years in the Big Apple, he'd increasingly participated in the nightlife the city had to offer. He could no longer bounce back as quickly or as easily as he once had from all the damage that had been done to his body. In the end, Mickey missed ninety-seven games, well over half of the season.

But Mickey being Mickey, he still made the most of those games, with a strong season average of .314 and fifteen home runs. The Yankees held it together and made it back to the World Series, going up against an old rival with a new home— the Dodgers, who had moved to Los Angeles, California. The Yankees had taken six of the seven series in which they'd battled the Brooklyn Dodgers. Would the odds hold out? Or would the Dodgers' new home base make the difference? The question was answered soon—too soon for Mickey as his team was swept by the Dodgers in four straight games. Ouch.

Mickey returned in 1964, hoping to set things right. At thirty-three years old, in his fourteenth year with the Yankees and after too many injuries to count, Mickey hit .303, thirty-five home runs, and 111 RBIs. Most incredible was the homer on August 12 at home in Yankee Stadium, when Mickey hit the longest measured drive in Yankee Stadium history. The ball soared an unbelievable 502 feet to center field.

TAPED LEGS

Many fans never realized what Mickey went through to play after his debilitating injuries. Before every game, Mickey had his legs wrapped thickly in tape and bandages from ankle to midthigh. After observing the taping ritual once, Cleveland Indian Early Wynn said, "Now I'll never be able to say enough in praise. Seeing those legs, his power becomes unbelievable." Wynn, by the way, was the pitcher who gave up the most home runs to Mickey—a total of thirteen!

With Mickey leading the charge, the Yankees once again owned the American League pennant and prepared themselves for the fight to reclaim their world champion title. The St. Louis Cardinals had something to say about that, and the teams traded off the first two games of the World Series, winning one apiece.

Game three belonged to Mickey. With a 1–1 score at the bottom of the ninth, Mickey came to bat, knowing it was up to him. He faced the Cardinals' pitcher, Barney Schultz, and guessed what kind of ball was heading his way. Then he turned to teammate Elston Howard and told him to go ahead and get changed because he was ending the game then and there.

True to his word, Mickey hit the first ball Schultz sent his way, burying it deep in the right-field stands. Another game-winning homer from Mickey! The Yankees were up two games to one. With that home run, Mickey's sixteenth in a World Series match, he'd also broken a record set by Babe Ruth.

Just to make sure his new record was secure for a long time, Mickey hit another two homers in the series, bringing his total to eighteen. He also drove in eight runs, bringing his World Series total to forty RBIs, another record. His hard work helped stretch the series to seven games, and it was during the crucial seventh game that Mickey knocked in that eighteenth home run. However, the Cardinals managed to pull off a 7–5 victory, grabbing the championship title out of the Yankees' reach.

The disappointment would grow for Mickey in later years as it became clear that 1964 had been the closest he'd come to one last World Series win. The following year was hard for both Mickey and the Yankees. Mickey's stats dipped below even those of his rookie season in 1951, and the team dropped to sixth place in the league. "Things just seemed to fall apart after [the 1964 season]," said Whitey Ford. In particular, Ford noted, the players of the great Yankee dynasty were growing older, and their bodies showed it.

But the fans still believed in Mickey, and on September 18, 1965—Mickey's 2,000th game—Mickey Day was celebrated at Yankee Stadium. The stands were packed to capacity, and Mickey was showered with gifts, including a new car, a mink coat for Merlyn, and a 100-pound salami! Joe DiMaggio even flew into town to introduce Mickey, telling fans, "I'm proud to introduce the man who succeeded me in center field."

❝*Mickey Mantle was everyone's hero. He was who you wanted to be.*❞

—ACTOR BILLY CRYSTAL,
A LIFELONG FAN OF MICKEY AND THE SPORT OF BASEBALL

Mickey walked onto the field with Merlyn and their children, his heart full of gratitude for all the support the fans were showing. "I just wish I had fifteen more years with you," Mickey told them.

As much as he knew that wasn't possible, Mickey still hoped to play for as many more years as he could. His body never stopped making it hard for him, however. In November he was playing football at home with his brothers Ray and Roy and son Mickey Jr. when he injured his right shoulder. It was time for more surgery, and Mickey wasn't even sure he'd make it for another season. But he was back in New York in 1966 and even improved slightly on his 1965 numbers.

The Yankees opened the 1966 exhibition season in Houston's new Astrodome, the first domed stadium in the world. Mickey wasted no time becoming the first player to hit a home run in a domed stadium.

Not only was Mickey still giving everything he could on the field, but he had truly taken on the role of leader off the field as well. During the mid-1960s, the Yankees experienced repeated turnovers in management after Ralph Houk was promoted. The team went through a series of short-lived managers—including Yogi Berra—none of whom seemed to be the right fit. Throughout this time Mickey encouraged his teammates, kept their hopes up, and did his best to make them feel included and important. Steve Whitaker, a player who started with the Yankees in 1966, remembers being terrified to play alongside the man he'd grown up idolizing. But on Whitaker's very first day, Mickey came and welcomed him. And it didn't stop there. "There were many times when I was down on myself, but Mickey would invite me to have dinner with him," Whitaker recalls. "He told me how he had gone through the same things, tried to help me raise my spirits."

To show gratitude for Mickey's leadership and remind him how much he was needed, management held a Mickey Mantle Fan Appreciation Day in 1966. But even with Mickey's efforts, it was still a difficult transition period for the Yankees. The season ended with the team a heartbreaking last in the American League.

Mickey appeared in a total of 2,401 games, more than any player in the history of the Yankees franchise.

By 1967 Mickey knew his years playing baseball were winding down. Whitey Ford retired in the second month of the season, and Mickey was soon switched to first base to reduce the strain on his legs. He was reunited there with Ford in 1968, when the pitcher came on board as a first base coach. The reunion wasn't altogether happy for Ford. "One of the sad things about coaching first base was that I was witnessing, firsthand, the demise of Mickey Mantle as a ballplayer," Ford said. Before Mickey left, he made sure to rack up a few more accomplishments. On May 14, 1967, he hit his 500th homer, becoming the sixth player ever to reach that mark. And he wasn't done yet—his final home run, on September 20, 1968, gave him a career total of a whopping 536.

Mickey finally announced his retirement from baseball on March 1, 1969, after debating with himself until the very last second over whether his body could handle another season.

❝I remember standing at third base one time . . . and [Mickey] hit a ball just to my left, and it was hit so hard I couldn't react to it. I mean, you're gonna react in one way or another on almost anything hit your way, but that ball was by me before I could move a muscle.❞

—TEAMMATE BOBBY MURCER, DESCRIBING A MOMENT DURING MICKEY'S LAST SPRING TRAINING, IN 1968

Saying good-bye to a game that had been in his blood since he was just hours old was one of the hardest moments of his life. It was second only, he admitted, to the day his father died. In a way, it was like saying good-bye to his father all over again. As Mickey told the press and his fans, "I just can't play anymore."

The third Mickey Mantle Day was held that June, and his number 7 jersey was officially retired. Deeply moved, Mickey remembered the speech Lou Gehrig had given after his retirement in 1939, after he'd been diagnosed with a terminal illness. "I never knew how a man who was going to die could stand here and say he was the luckiest man in the world," Mickey shared with the crowd, "but now I think I know how Lou Gehrig felt."

As sad as Mickey was to be leaving baseball, he was also bursting with pride and happiness over his years with the Yankees. "Playing eighteen years in Yankee Stadium . . . is the best thing that could happen to a ballplayer," he said. His one regret was that the lower averages during his final years had brought his lifetime average down to .298, keeping him from going down as the .300 hitter he had been for the majority of his career.

But Mickey's glory had never been about the numbers on paper. It was about his ability to explode at bat with unmatched power or to fly across the field at unimaginable speed. It was the pure thrill of hearing Mickey's bat crack against a ball and watching the ball soar to impossible heights. It was his absolute devotion to giving his blood, sweat, and tears to his team, playing through devastating injuries as if he weren't human. Mickey embodied the ability to break the limits of his very humanity, inspiring the fans to believe in the unbelievable.

---

66 There should be a special vocabulary to describe Mickey Mantle on the sports page. . . . He has to be the greatest athlete of these times.99

—SPORTSWRITER JIMMY CANNON IN 1966

At times Mickey really *did* feel superhuman, and coming back down to earth after his retirement was a shock to the system. His heart never left baseball, and in 1970 he accepted a coaching position with the Yankees as a way to stay involved. But he was the first to admit that he wasn't cut out for the job and didn't stay very long.

After leaving the coaching position, Mickey struggled to find something to do that felt meaningful. His marriage to Merlyn had continued to have problems over the years, and while the two never divorced, they eventually separated. Mickey did enjoy the chance to grow closer to his sons, however, and shared with them the love for baseball his father had once shared with him.

In 1974 Mickey was finally eligible, after five years in retirement, to be elected to baseball's Hall of Fame, and he became the *seventh* player (lucky number seven!) ever to be elected the first year he could, receiving 322 of the 365 votes cast. Even better, Whitey Ford made it in the same year, so Mickey and Whitey got to enjoy the moment side by side.

"It was all I lived for, to play baseball," Mickey said. And Mutt Mantle would have been proud because Mickey lived one amazing baseball player's life!

Epilogue

Everyone's Hero

After the excitement of his Hall of Fame induction, Mickey returned to his life at home with his family. He finally found some success and satisfaction when the baseball memorabilia business took hold. He couldn't believe how many fans still clamored for anything signed by the great Mick himself! Mickey would proudly travel to conventions and signings, usually with at least one of his sons at his side.

Part of the reason Mickey had spent so many of his Yankee nights out on the town—and so few of the days rehabilitating his injuries—was that he always believed in living for the moment. He took it for granted that his life would be cut short one day by Hodgkin's disease, just like most of his male relatives. But the disease never did strike him. Instead it struck his son Billy in 1977, when Billy was just nineteen years old. With treatment, Billy managed to live until 1994, but his death at the age of thirty-six hit Mickey very hard.

After years of abuse both on and off the field, Mickey's health was also suffering by this time. In 1993, with the help of his family, Mickey acknowledged that he had a drinking problem and sought help to turn himself around. One of his proudest lifetime accomplishments was conquering the problem, but unfortunately the damage had already been done. This time Mickey's sheer willpower and determination weren't enough to overcome his body's limitations. In the spring of 1995, Mickey was diagnosed with advanced liver cancer. Initially it seemed that a liver transplant would help, but soon after he received the transplant, the new liver became diseased as well, and the cancer spread to other organs.

Mickey died on August 13, 1995, leaving a family and nation to mourn him. He had spent his final months getting out an important message. Knowing he'd inspired many kids as an athlete, he hoped he could point fans away from the dangers of alcohol. In a news conference after his surgery, looking weak and ill, Mickey pointed to himself and said, "I'd like to say to kids out there, if you're looking for a role model, this is a role model. Don't be like me."

Mickey also spread the word about the importance of organ donation. Although it had not saved him, an organ transplant could be a lifesaving option for many, and Mickey made sure the public understood this. And just as the country had once watched every play he made, they listened to every word he spoke. After Mickey's announcement, organ donations suddenly increased across America, leading sportscaster Bob Costas to say in Mickey's eulogy, "Our last memories of Mickey Mantle are as heroic as the first."

In his final moments, Mickey was proud to know that he was once again a hero. To many people, he always had been.

PERSONAL STATISTICS

Name:

Mickey Charles Mantle

Nicknames:

The Commerce Comet, The Switcher, The Mick

Born:

October 20, 1931

Died:

August 13, 1995

Height:

5' 11"

Weight:

195 lbs.

Batted:

Switch-hitter

Threw:

Right

BATTING STATISTICS

Year	Team	Avg	G	AB	Runs	Hits	2B	3B	HR	RBI	SB
1951	NYY	.267	96	341	61	91	11	5	13	65	8
1952	NYY	.311	142	549	94	171	37	7	23	87	4
1953	NYY	.295	127	461	105	136	24	3	21	92	8
1954	NYY	.300	146	543	129	163	17	12	27	102	5
1955	NYY	.306	147	517	121	158	25	11	37	99	8
1956	NYY	.353	150	533	132	188	22	5	52	130	10
1957	NYY	.365	144	474	121	173	28	6	34	94	16
1958	NYY	.304	150	519	127	158	21	1	42	97	18
1959	NYY	.285	144	541	104	154	23	4	31	75	21
1960	NYY	.275	153	527	119	145	17	6	40	94	14
1961	NYY	.317	153	514	132	163	16	6	54	128	12
1962	NYY	.321	123	377	96	121	15	1	30	89	9
1963	NYY	.314	65	172	40	54	8	0	15	35	2
1964	NYY	.303	143	465	92	141	25	2	35	111	6
1965	NYY	.255	122	361	44	92	12	1	19	46	4
1966	NYY	.288	108	333	40	96	12	1	23	56	1
1967	NYY	.245	144	440	63	108	17	0	22	55	1
1968	NYY	.237	144	435	57	103	14	1	18	54	6
	Totals	.298	2,401	8,102	1,677	2,415	344	72	536	1,509	153

Key: **Avg:** batting average; **G:** games; **AB:** at bats; **2B:** doubles; **3B:** triples; **HR:** home runs; **RBI:** runs batted in; **SB:** stolen bases

FIELDING STATISTICS

Year	Team	Pos	G	C	PO	A	E	DP	FLD%
1951	NYY	OF	86	145	135	4	6	1	0.959
1952	NYY	3B	1	4	1	1	2	0	0.500
1952		OF	141	374	347	15	12	5	0.968
1953	NYY	SS	1	0	0	0	0	0	-.—
		OF	121	338	322	10	6	2	0.982
1954	NYY	2B	1	2	2	0	0	0	1.000
		SS	4	10	5	5	0	1	1.000
		OF	144	356	327	20	9	5	0.975
1955	NYY	SS	2	4	4	0	0	0	1.000
		OF	145	385	372	11	2	2	0.995
1956	NYY	OF	144	384	370	10	4	3	0.990
1957	NYY	OF	139	337	324	6	7	1	0.979
1958	NYY	OF	150	344	331	5	8	2	0.977
1959	NYY	OF	143	375	366	7	2	3	0.995
1960	NYY	OF	150	338	326	9	3	1	0.991
1961	NYY	OF	150	363	351	6	6	0	0.983
1962	NYY	OF	117	223	214	4	5	1	0.978
1963	NYY	OF	52	102	99	2	1	0	0.990
1964	NYY	OF	132	225	217	3	5	1	0.978
1965	NYY	OF	108	174	165	3	6	0	0.966
1966	NYY	OF	97	174	172	2	0	0	1.000
1967	NYY	1B	131	1,188	1,089	91	8	82	0.993
1968	NYY	1B	131	1,286	1,195	76	15	91	0.988
	Total		2,290	7,131	6,734	290	107	201	0.985

Key: Pos: position; G: games; C: chances (balls hit to a position); PO: put outs; A: assists; E: errors;
DP: double plays; FLD%: fielding percentage

BIBLIOGRAPHY

Castro, Tony. *Mickey Mantle: America's Prodigal Son.* Washington, D.C.: Brassey's, 2002.

Falkner, David. *The Last Hero: The Life of Mickey Mantle.* New York: Simon & Schuster, 1995.

Gallagher, Mark, and Neil Gallagher. *Mickey Mantle.* New York: Chelsea House Publishers, 1991.

Mantle, Mickey, and Phil Pepe. *My Favorite Summer 1956.* New York: Doubleday, 1991.

Mantle, Mickey, with Herb Gluck. *The Mick.* Garden City, NY: Doubleday, 1985.

Sloate, Susan. *Hotshots: Baseball Greats of the Game When They Were Kids.* Boston: Little, Brown, 1991.

WEB SITES

Official Mickey Mantle Web Site
www.themick.com
This site is loaded with facts, stats, quotes, photos, and links on Mickey.

New York Yankees: The Official Site
www.yankees.com
This is the official Web site of the New York Yankees. It includes a special section for young baseball fans.

INDEX

103